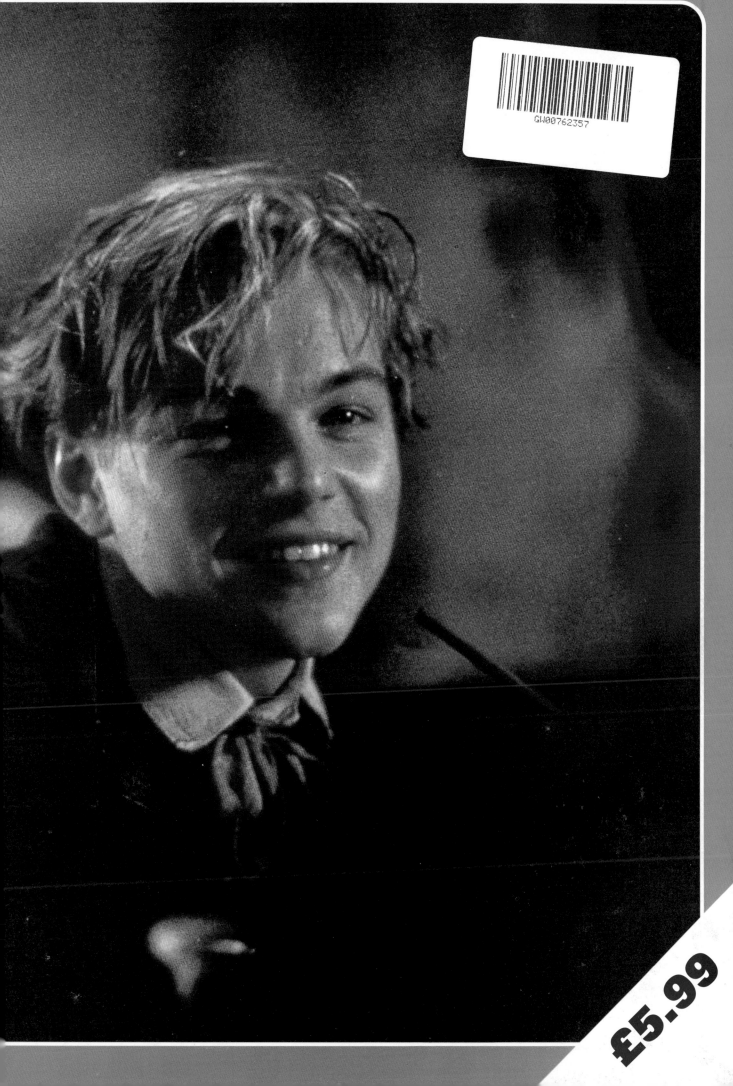

£5.99

Written by Anthony Laurence
Designed by Jason Bazini

Photographs supplied by All Action, Capital Pictures, Famous, London
Features International Ltd, The Movie Store Collection

Published by
Grandreams Ltd
435-437 Edgware Road
Little Venice
London W2 1TH

Printed in Belgium

THE TOTALLY 100% UNOFFICIAL LEONARDO DiCAPRIO SPECIAL

CONTENTS

'I'm the King of the

World!'

'I'm the King of the World' is a now famous line spoken by Leonardo DiCaprio's character 'Jack Dawson' in the mega-movie *Titanic*. It is delivered as Jack stands, arms outstretched, on the prow of the giant ship as it surges across the Atlantic Ocean.

Rarely has a line spoken by an actor in a movie so pointedly translated itself into his real life situation.

Following in the wake of *Titanic's* phenomenal success, film fans all over the world have gone overboard for the charismatic young star.

Sure, Leonardo DiCaprio is as handsome, sexy and charming as any pop idol of recent years. But he has a lot more going for him than that. The quality that has taken him all the way to the top, is an original and genuine talent.

Yet Leo did not study acting in the conventional 'drama school' sense – he learned his craft by actually performing in front of the camera.

Polish film-maker Agnieszka Holland, who directed him in *Total Eclipse*, said he is, '...like a medium...he opens his body and mind to receive messages coming from another person's life.'

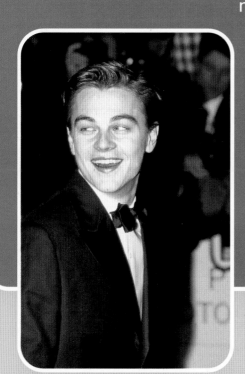

He is a natural actor and the movie camera loves him – when he is on screen it is virtually impossible to take your eyes off him.

This Totally 100% Unofficial Special examines the life and career of Leonardo DiCaprio, the terrific young actor who is Hollywood's hottest heart-throb – and the King of the Movie World...

Son of
HOLLYWOOD

Way back in 1974 George DiCaprio and his pregnant wife, Irmelin, were visiting George's homeland, Italy. They found themselves in the Uffizi Gallery in Florence, gazing up at a painting by Leonardo da Vinci. At that precise moment the baby began kicking inside his mother's womb.

George felt this was a wonderful sign and declared that, if a boy, the child would be named 'Leonardo', after the great Renaissance artist whose work hung before them. ▶

FLASHBACK – 1974

5 February
Millionaire's daughter Patty Hearst is kidnapped in California

8 February
Skylab astronauts return home after spending eighty-four days in orbit

6 March
Labour wins British General Election and Harold Wilson begins his third term as PM

29 March
The US Mariner 10 space probe captures close-up photographs of planet Mercury

30 March
Red Rum wins the British Grand National for a second time

3 April
The Sting, starring Paul Newman and Robert Redford, wins Best Picture Oscar in Hollywood

13 June
Twenty-five year-old Prince Charles makes his maiden speech in the House of Lords

30 June
Soviet ballet dancer Mikhail Baryshnikov defects to the West while on tour in Canada

7 July
West Germany win the World Cup final, beating Holland 2-1

8 August
US President Richard Nixon resigns in the wake of the 'Watergate' scandal

9 August
Gerald Ford is sworn in as the new US President

14 September
Giant pandas Chia-Chia and Ching-Ching arrive at London Zoo

1 October
British boxer John Conteh wins world light-heavyweight crown

11 November
Leonardo DiCaprio is born, in Los Angeles, California!!!

12 November
Lord Lucan goes missing in England

A confident smile from the young Leonardo DiCaprio

LEO FACT
With his father in the comics business, young Leo naturally gathered a large collection of comic books throughout his childhood. Among his favourites was the *Superman* series

Irmelin was German, and had first arrived in the United States as a young girl. She and George had been together for around ten years, having first met in college in New York. They lived a Bohemian lifestyle – George was a dedicated hippie who had enjoyed the 'Swinging Sixties' and had once shared a home with various members of a band called the Velvet Underground.

In New York, George was the creator and distributor of a well-known underground comic called *Baloney Moccasins*. He continued in the comics and alternative literature business when he and Irmelin moved west to Los Angeles.

The DiCaprio's child was born on 11 November 1974 in Los Angeles. The baby was a boy and, thanks to the 'sign' in the Uffizi Gallery, he was duly named Leonardo Wilhelm DiCaprio, the 'Wilhelm' coming from the German side of his family.

As the child grew up he would become known to one and all as 'Leo'. George and Irmelin's marriage broke up before Leo's first birthday. But they decided to remain friends and agreed they would both give their son all the love and attention he would need.

LEO FACT
The family name 'DiCaprio' is descended from the beautiful island of Capri, which lays a few miles off the Amalfi coast in Italy.

Mother and child lived in a rough area nicknamed 'Syringe City', near Hollywood Boulevard. It was there that young Leo would witness at first hand some pretty intense lowlife scenes involving drug pushers and addicts – scenes that would steer him away from the drug scene for life.

Later Irmelin and Leo moved to the more salubrious area of Los Feliz in East Hollywood.

The boy also spent a great deal of time with his father who later settled with another woman, Peggy Farrar, a professional bodybuilder. Peggy already had a son called Adam whom Leo calls his 'brother'.

On several occasions Irmelin took Leo to Germany to visit her parents, known to the boy as 'Oma' and 'Opa'. Being a quick learner, and with Irmelin's help, Leo quickly picked up the language and now speaks German fluently.

Although he had the face of an angel, little Leonardo DiCaprio was far from angelic. For instance, as an infant he refused to go to a day-care centre, therefore ▶

Leonardo out on the town with his mother, Irmelin

Irmelin had decided to find work as a child-minder so that her son could stay with her during the day.

His upbringing was unconventional to say the least, yet it had a truly positive effect on him. Unlike most kids he could never rebel against his parents and says: 'I didn't exactly grow up in a hippie family, but I guess you couldn't call us "Apple Pie and Republican" either. I mean, my parents were the rebellious ones, not me. Whatever I did would be something they'd already done...I don't think my parents would be shocked by anything I did, because they are so laid back.'

Among the youngster's chief interests was a love for animals of all kinds. He had a Rottweiler called Rocky who he once described as 'one of the most unfortunate dogs in the world'.

Rocky, the runt of the litter, had epilepsy and was prone to seizures. His medication made him overweight and he was tired all the time. It was discovered that the poor animal was also suffering from cancer and sadly he later died.

One of Leo's earliest ambitions was to become a travel agent so that he could visit endangered species around the world, and his love for animals continues to this day.

Leo attended the Centre for Enriched Studies and the Marshall High School, where he admits to being a pretty average student. In class he paid little attention to the lessons the teachers were attempting to cram into his head. But at break-time he came into his own, and could often be seen break-dancing or doing his famed impression of Michael Jackson, moon walk and all.

It was during a stay with his father that Leonardo first got the bug for performing in front of an audience. It happened at a performance festival in Los Angeles. Little Leo was wearing a red jump-suit and 'a tacky shirt', an image that remains a vivid memory for him.

George urged his son to get up on the stage. After a moment of shy hesitation he did so, and he began to tap dance. The audience loved it and egged him on. He got into the dance so much, that George eventually had to drag him off the stage.

Leo made his first TV appearance as a five-year-old on a kids' show called *Romper Room*. Unfortunately this would prove to be something of a false start to the phenomenal career of Leonardo DiCaprio – he was removed from the set because of his 'uncontrollable behaviour'.

It would be some years before he went in front of the cameras again. This time the inspiration was his brother Adam, who pursued an acting career (he was in the *Battlestar Galactica* TV series) for a while before opting for the military life.

When Leo learned that Adam had earned around $50,000 for appearing in a 'Golden Grahams' breakfast cereal commercial on TV, he decided he wanted some of the same. The magical figure stayed in his head and served as the driving force for this new ambition.

LEO FACT
Both Leonardo's parents continued to be involved with his phenomenal career. George vetted scripts on his son's behalf, while Irmelin handled the business side of things. He has said: 'I take advice from my agents and my parents, but ultimately I make the decisions.'

13

DiCAPRIO

DATA

Name: Leonardo Wilhelm DiCaprio
Birthplace: Los Angeles, California
Date of Birth: 11 November 1974
Star Sign: Scorpio

VITAL STATISTICS

Height: 6 ft
Weight: 10 st
Eyes: Blue
Hair: Blond-*ish*
Shoe size: 11 (US), 10 (UK)

FAMILY

Parents: George & Irmelin
Step-brother: Adam Starr

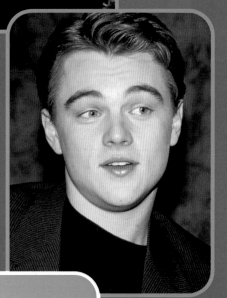

NICKNAMES

'The Noodle', 'Lee' or 'Dee'

BAD HABITS

Biting his nails
Twisting his hair

FAVOURITES

Movie Stars: Robert De Niro, Al Pacino, Meg Ryan, Jack Nicholson
Bands: Led Zeppelin, the Beatles, Pink Floyd
Book: *The Old Man and the Sea* by Ernest Hemingway
Sports: Basketball, Baseball
Food: Pasta, Cheeseburgers
Drinks: Diet Coke, Fruitopia, Lemonade
Colours: Black, green & purple

16

AN ACTOR'S LIFE FOR

LEO

At the age of 14, and with his parents' help, Leonardo DiCaprio found an agent and launched himself into the serious business of finding work as an actor.

And, in the time-honoured tradition of many an aspiring movie star before him, he set out on the endless round of auditions in and around the Hollywood area.

Eventually, he landed a job in a TV commercial for 'Matchbox' toys. He proved successful in that and was soon a regular at the studios. ▶

In all, Leonardo appeared in some twenty other commercials, advertising goods ranging from breakfast cereal to confectionery.

There were roles in educational and public information films too, including one sponsored by the US government and entitled *How to Deal with a Parent Who Takes Drugs.* Another early appearance by Leo came in Disney's *Mickey's Safety Club.*

Alongside these small successes came many rejections – and the strange suggestion from one agent that the young actor would stand a better chance of finding work if he changed his name to the ordinary sounding 'Lenny Williams'!

Leo now knew for sure that he wanted to pursue acting as a career, but he did not relish the anxiety and the pressures that went hand-in-hand with the territory. He confided these feelings to his father.

George, as cool and as laid-back as ever, turned to his son and said: 'Someday, Leonardo, it will happen for you. Remember these words: just relax.'

And as history shows – George was

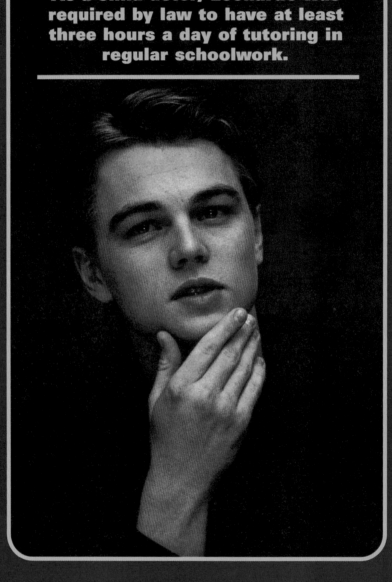

LEO FACT
As a child actor, Leonardo was required by law to have at least three hours a day of tutoring in regular schoolwork.

absolutely right.

But the boy's big screen success still lay a long way off in the future.

Leonardo's screen presence and his natural, unforced style of acting was eventually recognised by the industry professionals.

He was selected to appear as a troubled teenager in an episode of *The New Lassie* on TV.

Then he won another angst-ridden teenager role in *The Outsiders* – a TV spin-off from Francis Ford Coppola's 1983 movie that had helped launch the careers of 'brat-packers' Matt Dillon, Patrick Swayze, Rob Lowe, Tom Cruise and Emilio Estevez. Now the TV series helped Leonardo DiCaprio on his way.

Next up was a short spell in the popular soap opera *Santa Barbara*, in which Leonardo portrayed a teenager hooked on alcohol. This turned out to be an exhausting experience for the up-and-coming young actor.

The demands of TV soap opera included learning lines at relatively short notice, and then delivering them correctly

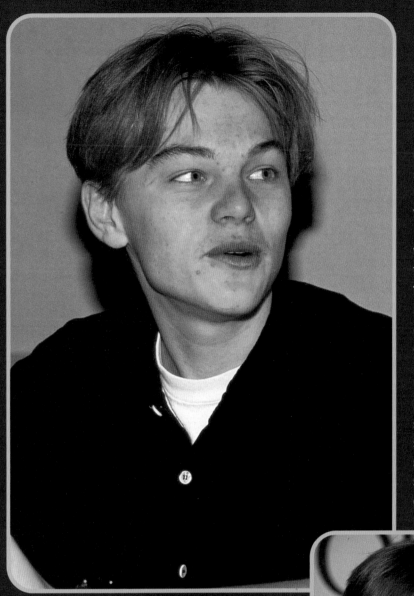

starring Steve Martin and Mary Steenburgen and directed by ex-*Happy Days* star Ron Howard. The film was also notable for an early appearance by future star Keanu Reeves.

Now NBC had developed the concept into a half-hour comedy series in which Leonardo played 'Gary Buckman', a reserved teenager with divorced parents.

He enjoyed both the role and working environment. And, for the first time, he was noticed by the teen magazines who snapped him up, hailed him as their latest idol and splashed his handsome face across their pages.

While all of this was going on, Leonardo was still a student. But he wasn't phased at all by the strange dual life of show-biz and schoolwork. Nor did his education suffer. Despite his reluctance to study, he knew the importance of gaining good grades.

Parenthood, while useful to Leonardo as it brought him to the attention of a nationwide audience, was not a ratings success. NBC pulled the plug on the show after just four months on air. Leonardo's next role marked his movie debut, even if it was an inauspicious one. The film was

without much rehearsal in front of the camera. (Like most soap opera actors Leo had his share of fluffed lines!)

When the job ended Leonardo packed the experience away in his memory bank – and decided that he would definitely *not* be pursuing a career in the soaps.

He made brief appearances in *A Circus Fantasy* and in the smash-hit comedy *Roseanne* – in which he met Sara Gilbert who played Roseanne's younger daughter 'Darlene' and who would later co-star in Leonardo's second movie *Poison Ivy*.

Leo's next regular role was also in a sitcom, but unfortunately it wasn't in the same league as *Roseanne*.

Parenthood had been a hit movie

Critters III, the third movie in a sequence that was inspired by the success of *Gremlins*. The 'Critters' in question were a gang of furry aliens who arrived on Earth via an asteroid and caused all sorts of destruction, devilment and devastation. ▶

20

In *Critters III* the aliens invade an apartment block and force the residents, including Leonardo's character 'Josh', onto the roof. It was the poorest movie of a poor series. In fact, Leo once called it 'The worst movie of all time' and prefers wisely to forget his association with it.

If *Critters III* did little to boost the budding career of Leonardo DiCaprio, his next TV role most certainly did boost it.

In 1991 he was cast as a new character called 'Luke Brower' in the long-running popular sitcom *Growing Pains*. This show had begun in 1985 and its plots revolved around the lives of the family of a psychiatrist 'Jason Seaver', portrayed by Alan Thicke. But the star of the show was Kirk Cameron who had played the Seaver's eldest son, 'Mike', since the show began.

Luke Brower was a homeless teenager who appeared in over twenty episodes during 1991-92 which marked the seventh and last *Growing Pains* season. Leo made a great impact in the role.

Once again he found himself featured heavily in the teen magazines and his mailbag constantly bulged with letters from adoring fans.

During the run of the show, Leonardo made his second big screen appearance in a small role in the thriller *Poison Ivy*, directed by Katt Shea Ruben.

This film was largely a comeback vehicle for seventeen year-old Drew Barrymore who, since winning fame as the child star of Steven Spielberg's *ET: The Extra-Terrestrial* in 1982, had encountered a certain amount of controversy while growing up.

In *Poison Ivy*, Drew Barrymore plays the title role of 'Ivy', a rebellious, sexy and scheming teenager who befriends 'Sylvie Cooper' (played by Sara Gilbert), and wheedles her way into the affections of Sylvie's wealthy father (portrayed by Tom Skerritt) then proceeds to dominate the family with horrific results.

By the time the film was released, Leo's role as a friend of Sylvie's was reduced to little more than a walk-on part in the opening scenes. But he really enjoyed the experience and was delighted to be reunited with his friend Sara Gilbert.

Meanwhile, *Growing Pains* continued towards closure. At one time there was talk that Leonardo's character would have his own spin-off series, to exploit his new-found popularity. But, in the end, the show simply closed and ended yet another chapter in the history of American television.

Nevertheless, *Growing Pains* had served to make Leonardo DiCaprio a true star of the small screen. Now he was ready to make another attempt at big-screen stardom.

LEO FACT
Leonardo remains loyal to his old friends. Known as the 'posse' they accompany him everywhere. He says: 'They help keep everything in perspective.'

Leo the
SCORPIO

A birthday on 11 November
makes Leonardo DiCaprio a Scorpio...

- **Scorpio** is the 8th sign of the zodiac

- **Scorpios** are incredibly sexy

- **Scorpios** are very intense

- **Scorpios** are very, very passionate and hot-blooded

- **Scorpios** are extremely loyal

- **Scorpios** like to take charge

- **Scorpios** can be rather jealous

- Watch out – there's always a sting in the tail of a **Scorpio!**

This Boy is
EXCEPTIONAL

As the final episodes of *Growing Pains* were being shot, Leonardo DiCaprio finally won the role that would propel him into the Hollywood stratosphere.

As a film-mad kid he had eagerly studied the films of his favourite actors – Al Pacino, Jack Nicholson and Robert De Niro. Now he was to find himself face-to-face with one of those big screen heroes. ▶

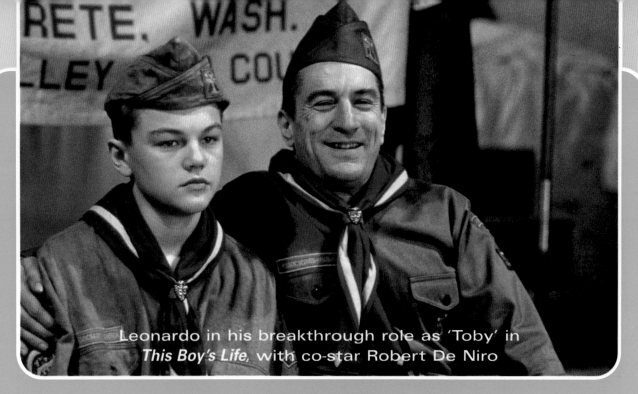

Leonardo in his breakthrough role as 'Toby' in *This Boy's Life*, with co-star Robert De Niro

The occasion would be a reading for the title role in the film adaptation of Tobias Wolff's best-seller *This Boy's Life*. The book was an autobiographical account of Wolff's growing-up – under the strain of an overbearing and abusive stepfather – in a remote town in Washington State in the late 1950s.

Leo was one of the first young actors to audition for the pivotal role of 'Toby'. So good was his initial reading of the part that the film's Scottish-born director Michael Caton-Jones could hardly believe his eyes and ears.

Nevertheless, the auditioning process continued and Michael Caton-Jones saw around 400 other young actors before whittling them down to a shortlist of the best candidates. Naturally, Leonardo's name was prominent on that list.

The next stage was a reading with the film's star who would be

Ellen Barkin played 'Toby's' mother in *This Boy's Life*

portraying 'Dwight Hansen', the brutal and controlling stepfather. That role would be played by none other than Leo's hero, Robert De Niro.

The part of Toby's mother, 'Caroline', would be played by Ellen Barkin, star of *The Big Easy* and *Sea of Love*. The film would initially follow mother and son as they travelled westwards across country.

While awed by the thought of meeting one of filmdom's top actors, Leonardo was not at all phased by the reading itself. He knew that the only way to make the role his own and beat off any competition, was to play it wholeheartedly.

Leo would later say of the reading: 'I didn't worry about what De Niro thought. I went in, looked him in the eye and got the part. I was confident, even though I'd never done anything like it before. Now I realise it was ignorant confidence – I had no idea.'

As far as Michael Caton-Jones and the film's producers were concerned, there was, in the end, no other young actor capable of carrying the role – and so they gave it to Leonardo DiCaprio.

It would prove to be a very wise choice.

Leonardo heard that he had got the part while on holiday with his mother in Germany – and naturally he was overjoyed. This was his Big Chance.

The shooting of *This Boy's Life* took place in Canada, in Utah and in the small town of Concrete, Washington, where Tobias Wolff had lived the life described in his book.

Partly thanks to the expert guidance of Michael Caton-Jones and the generous encouragement of Robert De Niro, the young DiCaprio produced a stunning natural performance as the teenage Toby. His success was also due to his own determination not to be over-awed by De Niro and Barkin. If the film was to succeed, then he had to put in a strong performance for himself.

While learning from his elder co-stars, Leonardo also seemed to have an instinctive grasp of many of the secrets of successful movie acting. Above all, he proved a great *reactor*, especially in scenes with Robert De Niro at his scariest.

Leo later said of the role, 'It was hard not to get

frightened. But I liked it when he scared me. It helped me to react.'

Michael Caton-Jones was delighted with the results and afterwards had nothing but praise for the rising young star. Leonardo had proven himself to be a true movie professional in his first major film.

On its release in 1993, *This Boy's Life* received some fine reviews. Leo's performance was recognised as a great piece of work and earned him his first awards – the New Generation Award from the Los Angeles Film Critics Association and the most Promising Actor Award from the Chicago Film Critics.

Suddenly Hollywood sat up and took notice of the talented teenager. Here was a kid to be reckoned with – a handsome young actor who was more than just a pretty face.

This time there would be no anxious waiting around for Leo to see what his next role would bring.

Before production of *This Boy's Life* was completed, he had agreed to appear as a mentally impaired teenager, in Swedish director Lasse Hallstrom's movie adaptation of Peter Hedge's novel *What's Eating Gilbert Grape?*

Leo had won the role ahead of other actors, thanks to his accurate and uncanny portrayal of a brain-damaged boy. There was a point, however, ▶

High drama for 'Arnie Grape'

Leonardo with *Gilbert Grape* co-stars Johnny Depp and Juliette Lewis

Leonardo as 'Arnie' in *What's Eating Gilbert Grape?*

when Hallstrom wavered over the choice – simply because Leo was too good-looking – but in the end the director went with his instincts and gave him the part. (Leo had to wear a special mouthpiece to slightly alter the shape of his face.)

The role of 'Arnie Grape', brother of 'Gilbert', was a brave choice for Leo – particularly so, when you consider that his good looks and recent success could easily have steered him towards a starry part in a glossier production. However, like his co-star Johnny Depp, who played the title role in *What's Eating Gilbert Grape?*, Leonardo seemed to be leaning towards a preference for 'quirky' roles.

If it was a brave choice, it was also a very shrewd one. Leonardo's portrayal of Arnie would prove to be even more remarkable than his performance alongside Robert De Niro and Ellen Barkin in *This Boy's Life*.

Heeding a lesson from the De Niro school of movie acting, Leonardo researched the part fully. At a home for mentally impaired children in Texas, he observed a certain unpredictability in one particular boy and decided to apply the observation to his portrayal of Arnie.

An intense moment between 'Gilbert' (Johnny Depp) and 'Arnie' (Leonardo DiCaprio)

The results were amazing. Leonardo stood out in what proved to be a touching, sometimes whimsical film, centred on Gilbert's efforts to keep his family together on a farm in Iowa.

So convincing was Leonardo's performance, that many who saw it believed that a mentally impaired actor had been cast in the role of the unfortunate Arnie.

The amazing believability of Leo's portrayal was recognised by the critics and by his fellow actors. It earned him a second Los Angeles Film Critics Association New Generation Award, a National Board of Review Award – and a Best Supporting Actor nomination in the 1994 Academy Awards.

The Oscar eventually went to Tommy Lee Jones for his role as the obsessed man-hunter tracking down Harrison Ford in *The Fugitive*. But Leonardo wasn't disappointed – or, if he was, he hid his feelings very well, by saying he was quite relieved at not having to make an acceptance speech in front of Hollywood's elite.

Believe it or not, he's shy about speaking in public. 'It's just this gut-wrenching fear of slipping up and doing something horrible,' he said.

LEO FACT
Leonardo has a scar on his right arm - the result of a close encounter with a deadly Portuguese man-of-war jellyfish.

The Things They Say About

LEONARDO

"He's a really brave actor."
Michael Caton-Jones, Director

"He's star material. In addition to depth, feel and range in his acting, he has a lot of sex appeal."
Lasse Hallstrom, Director

"He is like a man-child. He's both awkward and adult... He appeals to both men and women."
Renny Harlin, Producer/Director

"He's smart and talented beyond belief...He is the most gifted young actor I have ever seen."
Sharon Stone, Actress

"He was willing to take chances and you have to challenge yourself and the audience...Leo was always willing to go for it."
Agnieszka Holland, Director

"He is the most surprising young actor."
Agnieszka Holland, Director

"He's great, he's beautiful...So talented, so gifted and funny – everything you want in a person."
Diane Keaton, co-star in *Marvin's Room*

"He's always compelling. You can't watch anything else when he's acting."
Meryl Streep, co-star in *Marvin's Room*

"I thought he'd be the perfect Romeo, it was as simple as that."
Baz Luhrmann, Director

"With Leo it's like the Beatles."
Martin Brown, Producer

"He's probably the world's most beautiful looking man."
Kate Winslet, co-star in *Titanic*

"In life, he's a very humble, normal guy."
Jeremy Irons, co-star in *The Man in the Iron Mask*

THE TOTALLY 100%
UNOFFICIAL
Leonardo
DiCaprio
SPECIAL

Leonardo in *Marvin's Room*

Leonardo attends the premiere of *The Man in the Iron Mask*

The Road to
STARDOM

The Best Supporting Actor Oscar nomination for *What's Eating Gilbert Grape?* did wonders for Leonardo DiCaprio's career. But the young actor became very selective, deciding he would only appear in films that he actually believed in.

However, things didn't always go his way. For instance, he wanted to play the part of the 'Interviewer' in *Interview with the Vampire*, a role originally intended for River Phoenix, the young star of *Running on Empty* and *My Own Private Idaho,* who, sadly, died in October 1993. ▶

Leonardo auditioned for the part and by all accounts gave a stunning interpretation. Unfortunately for him, the film's producers felt he was a little too young for the role, which went instead to Christian Slater.

Leo's next venture was an odd one – a short black-and-white film entitled *The Foot Shooting Party* for producer/director Renny Harlin and directed by Annette Haywood-Carter. In it Leo plays a '70s rock star contemplating whether to accept the draft and go to war in Vietnam, or whether to avoid the army by shooting himself in the foot.

His next major role was a young gunslinger known simply as 'The Kid', in the western *The Quick and the Dead*, starring sexy Sharon Stone. Ms Stone was also the movie's co-producer and she knew that she wanted the hot young actor in her new film. However, she had to wait for his decision, as at first he wasn't sure he wanted to appear in a western.

Finally, with the advice of his agent and convinced that Sharon Stone truly believed he was the best actor for 'The Kid', he decided to accept the role.

Directed by Sam Raimi, *The Quick and the Dead* revolves around the revenge sought by Sharon Stone's character 'Ellen' for the killing of her father. The murderer and the object of her hatred is a man called 'Herod' who has become the mayor of a town called Redemption.

The setting for the showdown is the town's annual 'Quick Draw' competition organised and controlled by Herod.

The role of the ruthless mayor was played by Hollywood veteran Gene Hackman, another world renowned star from whom young Leo could hardly fail to learn. Also starring was Aussie actor Russell Crowe, who would later score a big hit as a hard-nosed cop in *LA Confidential*.

'The Kid' is Herod's estranged son – and as such he spends much of the movie attempting to impress his father with false bravado. He acts tough and cool and believes himself immortal, yet inside he is just an insecure youngster attempting to come to terms with the world around him.

The 'tough and cool' element of the role gave Leonardo a rare chance to display his comic talent. He also got to kiss sexy Sharon in the movie – but it wasn't a romantic kiss. After shooting a man, she grabs the Kid by his hair, kisses him roughly and then shoves him away. 'It was by no means a real kiss,' said Leonardo, who also later complained that the rough encounter actually hurt his lip!

Naturally the media made much of the kiss and soon stories were generated about an affair between the glamorous movie actress and her young co-star. Leonardo denied the allegations and insisted that he and Sharon were simply great friends who happened to work together. ▶

DiCaprio and Hackman – eye to eye

Leo with his co-stars in *The Quick and the Dead*:
Gene Hackman, Sharon Stone and Russell Crowe

The Kid's contribution to *The Quick and the Dead* ends when he is killed in a duel by the father he had so desperately wanted to impress. This was Leo's first ever death scene in a movie – and he played it to the hilt, giving the film a rare tear-jerking moment.

Jim Carroll's *The Basketball Diaries* was a best-selling memoir, written in the 1960s, but not published in book form until 1978. Its pages detailed Carroll's awful, harrowing descent from promising basketball player into a drug addiction hell from which he could see no escape.

Leonardo gave another stunning performance as 'Jim Carroll' in *The Basketball Diaries*

since his performance in *This Boy's Life*. The script was duly sent to Leo's agent. In turn, the young actor was knocked out by the story, and said it was the first script he'd read that was actually unputdownable.

Leonardo was a little concerned at first that Kalvert wanted to include Mark Wahlberg among the leading cast members. At the time Wahlberg was better known as rap star Marky Mark, and Leonardo felt that this might trivialise the movie. But the director was able to convince him that Wahlberg was absolutely right for the part of Jim's friend 'Mickey' – and Leo finally committed himself wholeheartedly to the project.

Carroll eventually fought off his demons and became a drugs counsellor.

Ever since its original publication *The Basketball Diaries* had been touted as a potential movie. Several young stars had wanted to play the lead role, including Eric Stoltz, Matt Dillon, River Phoenix and Johnny Depp. But for various reasons Hollywood had consistently shied away from the subject.

Then, in 1993, it came to the attention of producer Liz Heller and director Scott Kalvert, a name well-known on the music video scene.

Heller and Kalvert had been impressed by Leonardo DiCaprio ever

In the end Leo and Mark became firm friends and during filming in New York, they could often be seen out on the town together as they explored the club scene.

The Basketball Diaries also starred James Madio and Patrick McGaw as 'Jim' and 'Mickey's' basketball playing/drug-taking friends 'Pedro' and 'Neutron' respectively. Juliette Lewis (who co-starred with Leonardo and Johnny Depp in *What's Eating Gilbert Grape?*), portayed 'Diane'.

Playing Jim's long-suffering mother was Lorraine Bracco. Leo was mightily impressed by the co-star of the gangster

Leonardo as 'Jim' in *The Basketball Diaries*, with co-stars: (left to right) James Madio ('Pedro'), Mark Wahlberg ('Mickey') and Patrick McGaw ('Neutron')

epic *Goodfellas* for which she had been nominated for a Best Supporting Actress Academy Award. He was full of praise for her: 'Lorraine is the best woman I've ever worked with,' he said at the time. 'I kept messing up a scene and Lorraine was the only one who said "you can do it". '

As a movie *The Basketball Diaries* is a truly harrowing piece of work. The story, originally set in the '60s, is updated to the 1990s and centres on Jim's downward spiral into heroin-induced despair.

Leonardo's performance is powerful and intense – particularly when he pleads

with his mother for money, and in the scenes in which he experiences a gruelling 'Cold Turkey' treatment.

During his research for the role, Leo spent time with Jim Carroll himself, in an effort to achieve truth in his performance. The result was astounding – especially so since Leonardo does not do drugs.

The Basketball Diaries is a strong statement against the use of drugs. In the end the film delivers a positive and hopeful message as Jim, recovered from his habit, is seen reading some of his poetry to a rapt audience. ▶

LEO FACT
Leonardo is a great fan of the Los Angeles Lakers basketball team.

Leonardo DiCaprio, the fastest rising star of the 1990s, almost got to play the part of James Dean, the great movie icon of the 1950s.

Dean completed just three movies – *Rebel Without a Cause*, *Giant* and *East of Eden* – and his brooding angst-ridden presence in each of them, allied to his untimely death in a car crash at the age of twenty-four, made him a legend.

It is interesting to imagine what Leonardo would have made of the role. However, throughout negotiations he felt certain reservations about it. After all, no matter how good he was in the part, he would only be impersonating Jimmy Dean, thereby inviting inevitable comparisons.

In the end the project was shelved and – against the advice of his agent – Leo accepted the part of another rebellious young man, the hedonistic 19th century French poet Arthur Rimbaud, in *Total Eclipse*.

He also made a cameo appearance in the French film *Les Cent et Une Nuits* (One Hundred and One Nights) directed by Agnes Varda. This movie is about the history of cinema and called for the inclusion of a number of other brief appearances by such stars as Robert De Niro, Alain Delon, Catherine Deneuve, Gerard Depardieu, Harrison Ford, Daryl Hannah, Martin Sheen and Stephen Dorff.

Total Eclipse, made by Polish director Agnieszka Holland from a script by British dramatist Christopher Hampton, was shot in France. The film tells the story of the relationship between the young genius Rimbaud and an older poet, Paul Verlaine, portrayed by English actor David Thewlis.

Total Eclipse received poor reviews and was accused of pretentiousness. It includes a gay love scene which Leonardo found particularly difficult. He remarked, 'My stomach was seriously turning'. He is also seen naked for the first time on screen in *Total Eclipse* – in a scene that later became a selling point for its video release. 'Leonardo DiCaprio's Most Revealing Role' screamed a strapline on the cassette box.

In his next project, *Marvin's Room*, Leo found himself reunited with his *This Boy's Life* co-star, Robert De Niro. In the role of the troubled 'Hank' Leo also had a chance to play alongside two of cinema's finest leading ladies, Meryl Streep and Diane Keaton.

In *Marvin's Room*, which began life as a successful Broadway play by Scott McPherson, Leo plays 'Hank', the elder son of Meryl Streep's 'Lee'. At one point this troubled kid sets fire to his family home. Along with his mother and brother he moves in with his Aunt 'Bessie' (portrayed by Diane Keaton) who for seventeen years has looked after her father, 'Marvin'. Bessie is suffering from leukaemia and, according to her doctor (Robert De Niro) is in need of a bone-marrow transplant. The most likely match is, of course, her sister and her nephews. And so the stage is set for a tale of reconciliation and self-discovery by everyone involved.

Leonardo was particularly impressed with the double Oscar winner Meryl Streep. 'You feel this energy when she walks in,' he said, 'and everyone sort of becomes silent...When I did my first scene with her she was all over the place. I was thinking, "what's she doing?". It was so unlike anything I'd ever seen before. She did some wild things – and then you see it on film and everything she does seems completely natural and real.'

Working alongside and observing such high-calibre talent as Streep, Keaton and De Niro (again), simply added to Leonardo's store of movie acting knowledge – and helped him further along the road to stardom.

LEO FACT
Leonardo is often seen at fashion shows in places like Milan, Paris, Los Angeles and New York.

With David Thewlis
in *Total Eclipse*

Leonardo as the poet Rimbaud
in *Total Eclipse*

TOTALLY 100%
UNOFFICIAL

Leonardo was highly impressed
with his *Marvin's Room* co-star
Meryl Streep

Leo poses for the camera with
Marvin's Room co-star Diane Keaton

ROMEO

ROMEO!

It was one of the theatre's oldest texts that gave Leonardo DiCaprio his greatest cinema success before *Titanic* sailed into his life.

William Shakespeare's *Romeo & Juliet* is a play known all over the world. This tragic tale of two star-crossed lovers has been performed countless times. Every sentence of its text has been studied and analysed by millions of students. The plot had even inspired the great musical *West Side Story.* ▶

Furthermore, Shakespeare's classic has been filmed at least three times, most recently and most successfully in 1968, by Franco Zeffirelli and starring Leonard Whiting and Olivia Hussey in the title roles.

So, why do it again?

That was the question asked of himself by Australian director Baz Luhrmann.

The answer – it is a great story which could be brought right up to date while still retaining its eloquent Shakespearean dialogue.

Baz Luhrmann's movie making career had started with a bang. His film *Strictly Ballroom*, an award-winning smash hit in Australia and world-wide in 1992, was single-handedly responsible for a revival of ballroom dancing amongst today's youngsters.

Now Luhrmann turned his attention to updating William Shakespeare's play *Romeo & Juliet* – and right from the start he had Leonardo DiCaprio in mind for the role of 'Romeo'.

But Leo had reservations – until Baz explained his vision to him. This would be an action-packed, modern-day fantasy version of the old classic. It would be sexy, vibrant and full of youthful energy.

Actor and director got along well, and Leo was finally convinced that it was a great idea after all. He even appeared in a few test scenes for the movie which Luhrmann used to help persuade reluctant 20th Century Fox executives to invest in the project. On viewing this footage, the men in suits were well impressed and gave the project a green light.

The search for a 'Juliet' who could match Leonardo's 'Romeo' ended when Claire Danes auditioned for the role.

The young actress, who had starred on TV in *My So-Called Life*, was one of several who tried out for the part by reading with Leo. But she was the only one who looked him directly in the eyes as she spoke the famous lines. It was this forthright approach that persuaded Lurhmann and DiCaprio that she was definitely the right girl for the role. ▶

Director Baz Luhrmann's movie adaptation of Shakespeare's classic play *Romeo & Juliet* is a stunning visual treat

LEO FACT
When filming wrapped on *William Shakespeare's Romeo & Juliet*, Leonardo took a well-deserved break. He spent a wild time going to amusement parks – and doing other relaxing things, like Bungee Jumping!

Leonardo in action as a gun-toting Romeo

Baz Luhrmann did not alter the plot, but he changed the setting from Verona in Renaissance Italy, to the fictional present-day city of 'Verona Beach'. He made the Montague and Capulet families into two rival shady business syndicates. The characters drive around in open-topped limos, and handguns take the place of daggers and swords.

The movie was shot in Mexico, at a number of locations that made up the director's vision of the city of 'Verona Beach'.

William Shakespeare's Romeo & Juliet, as directed by Baz Luhrmann, is a fabulous visual treat full of light, colour and energy. Surprisingly, all of this does not detract at all from the story as it drives pulsatingly to its tragic conclusion.

Leo and Claire Danes are totally convincing as the two tragic lovers. You sense their passion for one another right from the moment that the couple first set eyes on one another.

Leonardo and Claire Danes at the premiere of *William Shakespeare's Romeo & Juliet*

LEO FACT
When Leonardo and his friends tried to view the famous *Mona Lisa* painting in the Louvre Museum in Paris, he was mobbed by screaming fans and had to be rescued by security guards!

Leonardo fully deserved the Silver Bear Best Actor Award given to him at the Berlin Film Festival, and the Blockbuster Award for Favourite Romance Actor.

Leonardo said the film was, 'The most emotional movie I've ever done. I had to be a wreck, a crying shambles, every other scene. To do that I had to take twenty minutes in the corner visualising horrible things...'

'Jack' (Leonardo) and 'Rose' (Kate Winslet) enjoy a dance
on board the ill-fated *Titanic*

TITANIC

On 10 April 1912, the White Star Line's SS *Titanic* set sail on her maiden voyage from Southampton. At 46,000 tons she was the biggest liner ever built at that time. En route to New York she was expected to challenge for the coveted Blue Riband, the prize awarded for the fastest crossing of the Atlantic Ocean.

On board the liner were some 2,220 passengers and crew, divided into three classes. In First Class were several millionaires, travelling in the lap of luxury. For these voyagers *Titanic* represented the height of ocean-going opulence. The ship's sumptuous decor and in-built elegance made them feel pampered and extra special, and helped to underline their standing in Edwardian society. ▶

In Third Class were many, many immigrants travelling in spartan steerage quarters, with few of the luxuries afforded to their upper-crust companions. Nevertheless they were looking forward to a new start in the promised land of the USA.

As the giant vessel surged westwards across the North Atlantic, everyone on board, of whichever 'class', must have felt privileged to be playing their own small part in a moment of history.

That question was answered in the most tragic of circumstances in the early hours of 15 April.

Despite warnings of icebergs in the vicinity, *Titanic* was sailing at top speed. It was before midnight on the 14th when she struck the iceberg that punctured her hull in several places. Water poured in, flooding the first five watertight compartments – and this ultimately proved to be too much, even for the engineering marvel of the age.

Sea water continued to surge through the hull of the giant ship, dragging

***Titanic* is a poignant movie that recreates all the horror of the biggest news event of 1912**

After all, they were on board the ship hailed as the engineering marvel of her age. With sixteen watertight compartments, and twelve watertight doors that could be operated from the bridge, the *Titanic* was said to be 'practically unsinkable'. And, even if the worse came to the worse and the unthinkable actually happened, then surely there would be enough room in the lifeboats for all to be saved?

the stern lower and lower into the sea. Yet, approximately two hours and 40 minutes passed before she finally split into two and sank to the ocean bed.

During that time, realisation of the disaster spread through the liner, slowly at first, and then with great panic.

More than 1,500 souls perished that night. Many went down with the ship. Others froze to death in the icy water. The majority of the survivors were from First Class – three millionaires, including the White Star Line's managing director, were said to have boarded the first lifeboat lowered to the sea.

Many steerage passengers found it impossible to get to the deck because iron partition gates were locked between the classes, thereby preventing their escape. For instance, of the 180 Irish passengers in Third Class, only twenty survived. And there was not only insufficient room in the lifeboats, there were simply *not enough* of them.

The sinking of the *Titanic* was a tragedy and a scandal.

It is ironic that the world's most unsuccessful ocean liner should provide material for the world's most expensive and ultimately most successful film.

Yet the story of the SS *Titanic* and her watery fate had fascinated film-makers ever since 1912. The first *Titanic* movie was *Night and Ice*, which appeared just a few months after the disaster and was roundly condemned as being in poor taste.

In 1958 *A Night to Remember* told the story from the perspective of Second Officer Herbert Lightoller, who first raised the alarm on sighting the iceberg. Kenneth More starred as Lightoller in this black-and-white epic which was the best retelling of the story – until James Cameron's 1997 version sailed into view.

Raise the Titanic (1980) was a complete disaster, both critically and at the box-office. This film told the tale of a team of divers attempting to salvage certain rare minerals from the wreckage. Its producer, Lord Grade, famously quipped it would have been cheaper to lower the ocean than to raise the *Titanic*!

The *Titanic* story had long fascinated James Cameron, the Canadian-born writer/director of such smash hits as *The Terminator, Terminator 2: Judgement Day, The Abyss* and *True Lies*. Each of those productions had demonstrated Cameron's mastery of popular cinema – but *Titanic* would prove to be the biggest challenge of his career.

Given the facts of the sinking, Cameron decided to humanise the events by placing at its heart the story of a shipboard romance that might have blossomed had the ship reached its intended destination.

For the two pivotal roles Cameron cast English actress Kate Winslet as 'Rose DeWitt Buketer' and Leonardo DiCaprio as 'Jack Dawson'.

To begin with Leo wasn't particularly interested in playing the part. 'I saw it as another doomed lover role,' he said, 'and I had just completed *Romeo & Juliet*. I wanted to try something really different.'

When director and actor met to discuss the role, Cameron suggested that Leo had only ever played misfits, '...and that I was afraid to tackle someone as normal as Jack Dawson in *Titanic*,' recalled DiCaprio.

That did it. Leo accepted the challenge and was finally won over by the romance in the script.

Kate Winslet had risen rapidly to stardom following a riveting appearance in *Heavenly Creatures*, a chilling true life story from New Zealand, and in the movie adaptation of the Jane Austen classic *Sense and Sensibility* for which she had received an Academy Award nomination.

Titanic would mark Leonardo's first appearance in a big budget, mainstream, blockbuster movie. It was quite a challenge and a huge responsibility for the two young performers whose shoulders would bear the weight of the ▶

Leonardo and Kate Winslet at the Golden Globe Awards

film. In the event both played their roles to perfection, adding an extra element of poignancy to the disaster that we know awaits the SS *Titanic*.

Jack is a poor American-born artist, who would not have been on board the ill-fated ship at all, had he not won tickets for himself and his friend, Fabrizio, in a game of poker.

cynical millionaire expects to embarrass the young artist while at the same time providing some amusement for his upper-crust friends.

But Jack is not put down, he responds to the conversation with wit and sensitivity and touches Rose's heart. He then invites her down into steerage where – in contrast to the sedate stuffiness of the

Rose, a rather spoilt rich girl, is engaged to social climbing millionaire 'Caledon Hockley', played by Billy Zane. At heart she is deeply unhappy at her situation and decides to throw herself overboard, only for Jack to save her in the nick of time.

In thanks for his timely intervention, Jack is invited by Hockley to dine at his First Class table – an event at which the

First Class restaurant – they enjoy a lively energetic dance and Rose lets her hair down for the first time in ages.

After that, their unstoppable whirlwind romance is underway and is intertwined with the slowly unfolding disaster that awaits the giant ship.

Wrapped around the events of 1912 is a modern-day story in which Rose, now 101 years-old, returns to the site of the ▶

TOTALLY 100% UNOFFICIAL

Leonardo attends the *Titanic* premiere in London...

sinking to help in the recovery of a precious diamond known as 'The Heart of the Ocean'.

Among the artefacts brought to the surface is Jack's miraculously preserved drawing of Rose, reclining on a chaise longue, naked – except for 'The Heart of the Ocean' around her neck.

It is from this point in the film that both the disaster and the love story between Jack and Rose are so brilliantly recalled.

To recreate the tragedy on celluloid was a massive undertaking, requiring the construction of a 750-foot-long replica of the 'unsinkable' ship at a location in Mexico, complete with a hydraulic system to simulate the actual sinking. Then there was the building of a set inside a tank containing millions of gallons of water – and incredible expertise in the fields of model making and computer generated imagery.

...and gets ready for the party afterwards!

While the film was in production, rumours spread that the $200 million-plus budget had spiralled out of control, that the project was over-schedule and that it was doomed to failure.

But when the film opened, James Cameron and his cast and crew had the last laugh. *Titanic* was a massive success and within weeks of its release had become the most successful movie of all time, even eclipsing Steven Spielberg's 1993 dinosaur epic *Jurassic Park*.

At the 1998 Academy Awards the film garnered a record fourteen Oscar nominations – and carried off eleven of them. This brilliant and well-deserved haul equalled the previous record set by *Ben-Hur*, way back in 1959.

Strangely, Leonardo DiCaprio was not listed among the Oscar nominees – yet it is he, and co-star Kate Winslet, who the audience remembers. The extraordinary love story of Jack and Rose is right there at the heart of *Titanic.*

As the epic three-hour, 24 minute film draws to its fateful conclusion, everyone in the audience is willing both Jack and Rose to survive so that they can share a life together.

Alas, it is not to be.

LEO
MANIA

Titanic's phenomenal success made its leading man world famous. It seemed that wherever Leonardo DiCaprio went he was greeted by a legion of screaming fans. Photographers followed him everywhere and his face appeared on countless magazine covers... Newspapers speculated wildly about his love life... His face adorned a million posters on a million bedroom walls... Web-sites devoted to Leonardo sprang up on the Internet... And when his next film, *The Man in the Iron Mask*, was released, the new phenomenon known as 'Leo-Mania' grew to even greater proportions. ▶

Leonardo in *The Man in the Iron Mask*

'And his new script has all the same themes of valour and passion and honour, as opposed to the typical machismo thing you see in a lot of films these days...The story is so complex, it has so many twists and turns and you really get wrapped up in what's happening.'

Leonardo plays the dual roles of the ruthless and arrogant 'Sun King', Louis XIV of France, and his identical twin brother, 'Philippe'. Philippe is imprisoned by Louis in the Bastille and condemned to live his life behind a hideous iron mask. Until, that is, the ageing Musketeers help to free Philippe from his mask and to put him on the throne in place of Louis.

In London, in March 1998, an estimated 20,000 fans turned up to see the young heart-throb arrive for the movie's premiere at a cinema in Leicester Square. Many had queued from early on the previous day to gain a good vantage point from which to catch a glimpse and snap a photo or two of their hero.

The Man in the Iron Mask is an adaptation of the famous Alexandre Dumas novel, scripted and directed by Randall Wallace who had previously written Mel Gibson's *Braveheart*, which won the Best Picture Oscar in 1995 (Wallace was also nominated in the Best Screenplay category).

What initially attracted Leonardo to *The Man in the Iron Mask* was its gripping script. 'Randy's *Braveheart* is one of my favourite films of recent years,' he said.

The Musketeers are portrayed by Jeremy Irons (as Aramis), John Malkovich (Athos), Gerard Depardieu (Porthos) and Gabriel Byrne (D'Artagnan) – another quartet of great

Leonardo contemplates the mask

Leonardo as 'Philippe', with John Malkovich as 'Athos'

talent from whom Leonardo would learn more of the tricks and techniques of his chosen profession. 'I didn't know if we would all mesh together,' he said. 'But as soon as we started working, it was a totally relaxed set. [We] just joked around like schoolboys.'

Anne Parillaud plays the 'Queen Mother', while Judith Godreche is 'Christine', a beautiful courtier wooed by the King.

For Leonardo the worst part of the filming process was having to wear that horrendous headgear. In fact, he hated it at first. 'It got claustrophobic and within ten minutes I could almost

bash my head against the wall in frustration...I realised if I was going to survive, I had to make the mask a part of my body. I wore it around for hours, all the time fighting off the urge to scratch my face off.'

Although short on historical accuracy, *The Man in the Iron Mask* is an entertaining romp, a lavish production with sumptuous sets and some fine acting. And once again Leonardo puts in a shining performance – this time wearing his hair at shoulder length – to keep his adoring fans more than happy.

If you look like Leonardo ▶

LEO FACT
Leonardo DiCaprio has become not only a world famous movie star, but also an extremely wealthy young man. He reportedly took a percentage of *Titanic*'s profits. The film went on to become the most financially successful movie of all time, grossing more than a billion dollars around the world!

Leonardo watches a playback with *The Man in the Iron Mask* director Randall Wallace

DiCaprio and if half the young women on the planet want to get to know you, then what's a red-blooded boy supposed to do? In parallel with his fast rising career, Leonardo has certainly earned himself a reputation as something of a ladies' man. He has expressed a preference for intelligent women with a good sense of humour.

His name has been linked – mainly by the news-hungry media – with a succession of beautiful models and actresses including Natasha Henstridge, Helena Christensen, Demi Moore, Liv Tyler, Gwyneth Paltrow, Alicia Silverstone, Amber Valetta, Naomi Campbell, singer Alanis Morisette and of course Kristin Zang, with whom he had a much publicised fifteen-month relationship.

LEO FACT
It was recently reported that Leonardo was offered an incredible $4 million to appear as a noodle-eating detective in a TV commercial to be shown only in Japan!

More recently it was reported that Leonardo was head-over-heels in love with glamorous twenty-year-old New Yorker Vanessa Haydon. The daughter of a prominent show-biz lawyer, Vanessa is known to be super intelligent and is tipped to be 'the supermodel of the new over themselves to sign you for their next big picture... Knowing that your face is familiar in almost every country in the world. Surely it's all got to go to the boy's head!?!

Yet, somehow, Leonardo seems to take fame and all its trappings in his

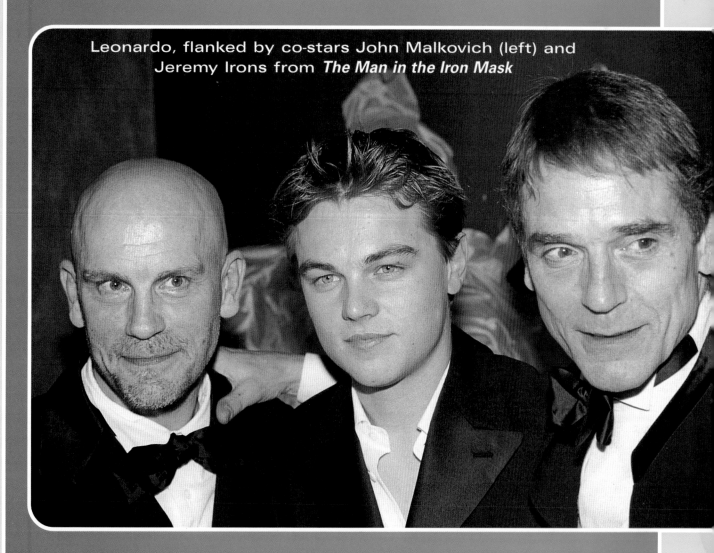

Leonardo, flanked by co-stars John Malkovich (left) and Jeremy Irons from *The Man in the Iron Mask*

millennium'. Could this be the Real Thing for Leonardo? Only time will tell.

Perhaps his *Titanic* co-star Kate Winslet best summed up his gentle appeal to females, when she said: 'I was expecting he'd be just another self-centred stud but he's not at all, even though he's absolutely gorgeous'.

So, being called 'absolutely gorgeous' and 'King of the Movie World'... Having movie producers falling stride. He does not appear to be big-headed at all, and he displays a remarkable lack of pretension and ego for someone in such an enviable position. This quality makes him all the more appealing to that ever-growing legion of fans.

Leo-Mania will no doubt blossom every time a new Leonardo DiCaprio movie is released.

Let's hope there are lots of them!

LEONARDO DiCAPRIO – CAREER DETAILS

TV APPEARANCES
Leonardo appeared in numerous TV commercials

EDUCATIONAL FILMS
Mickey's Safety Club
How To Deal With A Parent Who Takes Drugs

TV SERIES
Romper Room
The New Lassie
The Outsiders
Santa Barbara
A Circus Fantasy
Roseanne
Parenthood
(Leonardo appeared as regular character Gary
Buckman)
Growing Pains
(Leonardo appeared as regular character Luke Brower)

MOVIES

CRITTERS III
New Line Cinema
USA 1991, 89 mins
Director: Kristine Peterson
Cast: John Calvin, Aimee Brooks, Christian Cousins,
Joseph Cousins, William Dennis Hunt, Nina Axelrod,
Leonardo DiCaprio
* Available on video

POISON IVY
New Line Cinema
USA 1992, 89 mins
Director: Katt Shea Ruben
Cast: Drew Barrymore, Sara Gilbert, Tom Skerritt, Cheryl
Ladd, Leonardo DiCaprio
* Available on video

THIS BOY'S LIFE
Warner Brothers
USA 1993, 115 mins
Director: Michael Caton-Jones
Cast: Robert De Niro, Ellen Barkin, Leonardo DiCaprio,
Jonah Blechman, Eliza Dushku, Chris Cooper, Carla
Gugino, Zack Ansaley
* Available on video

WHAT'S EATING GILBERT GRAPE?
Paramount
USA 1993, 118 mins
Director: Lasse Hallstrom
Cast: Johnny Depp, Juliette Lewis, Mary Steenburgen,
Leonardo DiCaprio, Darlene Cates, Laura Harrington,
Mary Kate Schellhardt, Crispin Glover, Kevin Tighe
* Available on video

THE FOOT SHOOTING PARTY
Touchstone
USA 1994, 27 mins
Director: Annette Haywood-Carter
Cast: Leonardo DiCaprio

THE QUICK AND THE DEAD
Tri-Star/JSB Productions
USA 1995, 108 mins
Director: Sam Raimi
Cast: Sharon Stone, Gene Hackman, Russell Crowe,
Leonardo DiCaprio, Torbin Bell, Robert Blossom, Lance
Henriksen, Kevin Conway, Gary Sinise, Woody Strode
* Available on video

THE BASKETBALL DIARIES
Island Pictures/New Line Cinema
USA 1995, 100 mins
Director: Scott Kalvert
Cast: Leonardo DiCaprio, Lorraine Bracco, James Madio,
Patrick McGaw, Mark Wahlberg, Bruno Kirby, Juliette
Lewis, Ernie Hudson, Michael Rappaport
* Available on video

TOTAL ECLIPSE
Capital Films/Fine Line/Fine Line Features
USA 1995, 110 mins
Director: Agnieszka Holland
Cast: Leonardo DiCaprio, David Thewlis, Romane
Bohringer, Dominique Blanc, Nita Klein, James Thieree,
Emmanuelle Oppo
* Available on video

LES CENT ET UNE NUITS
(One Hundred and One Nights)
Cine-Tamaris/France 3 Cinema/Recorded Pictures
Company
France 1995, 101 mins
Director: Agnes Varda
Cast: Michel Piccoli, Marcello Mastroianni, Henri Garcin.
Cameo appearances by: Robert De Niro, Alain Delon,
Catherine Deneuve, Gerard Depardieu, Leonardo
DiCaprio, Stephen Dorff

MARVIN'S ROOM
Tribeca Productions
USA 1996, 98 mins
Director: Jerry Zaks
Cast: Meryl Streep, Leonardo DiCaprio, Diane Keaton,
Robert De Niro, Hume Cronyn

WILLIAM SHAKESPEARE'S ROMEO & JULIET
Bazmark/20th Century Fox
USA 1996, 120 mins
Director: Baz Luhrmann
Cast: Leonard DiCaprio, Claire Danes, Zak Orth, John
Leguizamo, Paul Sorvino, Brian Dennehy, Christina
Pickles, Harold Perrineau, Paul Rudd, Vondie Curtis-Hall,
Jesse Bradford, M. Emmet Walsh, Diane Venora, Miriam
Margolyes, Des'ree, Pete Postlethwaite
* Available on video

TITANIC
20th Century Fox/Lightstorm Entertainment/Paramount
Pictures
USA 1997, 194 mins
Director: James Cameron
Cast: Leonardo DiCaprio, Kate Winslet, Bill Paxton, Kathy
Bates, Billy Zane, Jonathan Hyde, Suzy Amis, David
Warner, Frances Fisher, Bernard Hill

THE MAN IN THE IRON MASK
United Artists
USA 1998, 132 mins
Director: Randall Wallace
Cast: Gabriel Byrne, Gerard Depardieu, Leonardo
DiCaprio, Jeremy Irons, John Malkovich, Anne Parillaud,
Judith Godreche